Th

BOYNE V Y

Book and Tape of

IRISH LEGENDS

Text by Brenda Maguire :: Illustrated by Robert Bates

Introduced by Dr. Patricia Donlon
and featuring
Kathleen Watkins · Niall Toibin · Ronnie Drew
Paul Acheson · Maxi · Marian Finucane

Published by
BOYNE VALLEY HONEY COMPANY

Contents

Produced by: Orla Tunney

Edited by: Myles McWeeney and Graham Stone

Origination by: First Generation Reproductions, Dublin 17

Printed by: Kellyprint Ltd, Dublin 17

First published in 1991 by the Boyne Valley Honey Company, Mell, Drogheda, Co Louth, Ireland.

ISBN 0 9517823 0 4

Here are some great stories – stories first told thousands and thousands of years ago, so long ago we've forgotten who wrote them or when they were written.

They were told by storytellers at fairs and firesides and later by grandmothers and fathers, uncles and sisters. The oldest people in the villages and towns told them to the youngest.

Sometimes these stories were written down in great books made of animal skins or even on tiny scraps of paper or copybooks.

Many of these old manuscripts and books can be found in our finest libraries, but now you can just curl up in your favourite corner or chair and listen to them again, read to you by some pretty famous people.

Some of the stories will give you goosepimples. Many will bring you to places that no aeroplanes go: to the Land of Many Colours, to the Well at the World's End. You don't need a passport, just your imagination.

And the best part? When you're finished you can listen and read them all, over and over again, as often as you like.

Patricia Donlon

Dr. Patricia Donlon

Director, National Library of Ireland.

The Wooing of Etáin

My mother told me this story and she heard it from her mother and now I'm telling it to you.

Long long ago, beyond the mist of time, there lived in the Land of Many Colours a young and beautiful princess called Etáin. Etáin was tall, with long soft hair that was yellow as gold and billowing as the curling clouds in the sky. Her eyes were clear as the running brook and blue as the sky on a bright summer's day. Her teeth were white as snow, her lips beautifully curved and red as winter berries and her lovely cheeks were pink and smooth.

There was no sport or craft at which she did not excel. When she spoke her voice was sweeter than the singing lark; when her long slender fingers plucked the strings of the harp all who heard the soothing music felt happy and peaceful.

Indeed, it is true to say that the good fairies were at her christening and endowed her with all the best and most precious gifts: love, generosity, gentleness, kindness.

When Etáin walked in the woods, the birds and the beasts kept her company. The thrush loved to sing a duet with her and the gentle deer searched her pockets for home-made sweetmeats which she always kept for them.

Etáin loved the sea and when she stepped into a coracle to go sailing the great whales, the black seals

ETAIN LOVED THE SEA

and the clowning porpoises made her laugh with their antics. The small fish came sliding and flickering by and the many creatures of the deep rose high into the air and dived, twirling around her craft.

Now, in the Land of Many Colours, time stands still. There is no sickness, no death. Food and drink are full and plenty. To wish for something is to possess it.

Etáin wished for love and her happiness was complete when she met Midir, the most charming and the most handsome prince in the Land of Many Colours. They fell in love and the feasting and merriment that followed their marriage lasted for a year and a day, the last day being better than the first. But, even in the Land of Many Colours, there can be a dark side to nature.

Fuamnach, a spoiled and evil princess, was jealous of Midir's love for Etáin. She tried every possible trick to turn Midir against his wife. But his love for Etáin was strong and, when Fuamnach's plans were foiled, her jealousy grew so intense that, in a fit of mad rage, she struck Etáin with a hazel rod. She turned her into a golden fly and banished her from the Land of Many Colours.

For ten long years, poor Etáin was tossed about on the high seas.

She was scorched by the sun and battered by the wind and, when it seemed that she must surely die of loneliness, a magic wind caught her and carried her far, far away from the Land of Many Colours, into the Land of Dark Shadows, which we call Earth. The golden fly came to rest on the window sill of a little thatched cottage in County Mayo on the west coast of Ireland. It was a beautiful morning in May. The birds were singing, high up in a clear blue sky. The lambs were frolicking on the mountainside and, inside the cottage, a young woman was happily spinning, a mug of fresh buttermilk beside her on the table. The little fly was enjoying the beautiful scene when a puff of wind blew it through the open window, across the room and into the mug. Before the woman could stop herself she had swallowed the milk, fly and all.

Some time later the young woman gave birth to a baby girl, with soft golden hair and clear blue eyes.

"What shall we call her?" the young woman asked her husband and, as if in answer, the wind whispered "Etáin, Etáin."

And so the baby was called Etáin. She was a happy carefree child, beautiful and talented and loved by all.

More than anything else, she liked to sit on the rocks overlooking the wild ocean and dream her dreams.

"Some day" she would whisper to her pet dog, Misty, "my prince charming will come riding across the waves on a white charger and carry me off to a land beyond all dreams, where no one grows old and the sun always shines." And Misty would bark knowingly, as if to say, "And will you take me with you?"

One glorious summer's day, when the beautiful Etáin was nearing her 17th birthday, Eochy, King of Ireland, came riding by. Etáin was chasing a golden butterfly through the ripening cornfields, Misty at her heels. She wore a purple cloak held with a silver brooch. Her golden hair blew in the wind.

The King fell instantly in love with her and, soon after, took her to Tara to be his Queen.

Eochy built a wonderful castle for Etáin. It had three hundred and sixty-five windows, one for every day of the year, and magnificent green marble turrets inlaid with gold, silver and precious stones. Walls were hung with splendid tapestries and each night the banqueting hall was filled with the sound of music, dancing and storytelling.

When Etáin heard tales of how Oisín went riding on a white horse to Tír na nÓg with Niamh of the Golden Hair, she felt a strange tug at her memory. Pictures of a land most beautiful to behold flashed past her mind – lovely colours shining on every side, chariots of gold and silver and bronze, a handsome prince called Midir, wild strawberries and honey cakes to eat and hazel mead to drink.

For a moment in time she remembered Tír na nÓg; then the dream was gone.

Early one morning, when Eochy and Etáin were out riding, they came to a glade where the sun shone and the earth was warm. They stopped to rest their horses and, as they did so, a fairy mist came down. When it lifted again, a stranger of noble bearing stood before

A stranger of noble bearing stood before them.

them. His golden hair reached to his shoulders and he wore a magnificent crimson mantle. A great brooch of burnt gold was pinned at his breast and he carried a silver chess-board, inlaid with priceless gems.

The stranger looked deep into Etáin's eyes and memories came flooding back to possess her: the Land of Many Colours, Midir, Fuamnach's jealousy. "Midir" she whispered "Is it really you?"

But the stranger was talking. "King Eochy, I challenge you to a game of chess, the winner to choose the stakes."

Etáin sighed and put her hand on the King's shoulder. But too late. Eochy loved a game of chess and had agreed to play.

Eochy made the first move. The players were evenly matched and, when it seemed that there might be stalemate, Midir made a foolish move and Eochy won the game.

The King asked for fifty snow-white horses which would be swift as the wind and tame as the deer, their nostrils wide, their hoofs slender. Even as he spoke, his wish was granted.

The King won the second and third games and, in turn, asked that four roads be built from Tara across Ireland – stretching north, south, east and west – and that the plains of Meath be cleared of stones and rocks. Once again he got what he asked.

A fourth time the pieces were set out and Midir and Eochy faced each other. Midir made the opening gambit and the game continued. Midir moved again, calling 'checkmate'. The King had lost the game.

"I demand a kiss from your Queen" Midir said.

Eochy knew that the stranger was no mortal man, but a promise made in good faith must be kept. He asked Midir to return to Tara in a month to claim his prize.

On the appointed day King Eochy ringed Tara with ten thousand warriors. All the doors and windows were locked and barred.

But locks and bolts could not hold Midir and, when he stood in their midst, a great sorrow overcame the King. He drew his beloved Etáin to his side.

Midir put his arms around the Queen and kissed her on the lips. At that instant, the great bronze roof of Tara opened up. As Eochy watched, Midir and Etáin rose up into the sky, transformed into two snow white swans. The swans circled Tara. Then, winging their way up into the heavens, they took the starry path out over the wild Atlantic Ocean to the Land of Many Colours.

The beautiful Etáin was never seen again.

The Well at the World's End

Once upon a time, there lived a certain King and Queen who had a son, called Brian. When Brian was only a baby his mother died. The King was heartbroken and would have died of grief but for the great love he had for the young prince.

Brian grew up to be a gentle, fun-loving boy and, when he was five years of age, his father married for a second time. At first the new Queen cared for her stepson with a mother's love but, gradually, she became jealous of the love the King had for little Brian. She had a son of her own, called Fergus, and she determined that he, and not Brian, would inherit the kingdom, so she plotted and planned how she could get rid of the young prince.

When Brian was seventeen years of age, his stepmother took to her bed and pretended to be dying. She said that the only thing that would cure her was a drink of water from the Well at the World's End, so she put geasa on Brian to go to the World's End and bring back the water. Now geasa are bonds that must be kept and poor Brian had no option but to agree.

"As you have put geasa on me I must accept", he said to his stepmother. "But in turn I put geasa on you. Order your son Fergus to come with me."

The Queen was distraught, since she knew that there was little hope of the young men ever returning, but Brian had trapped her and she could not refuse.

Early next morning they set off for the Well at the World's End.

Far, far away they rode, farther than I can tell you and twice as far as you can tell me. They did not stop for food or drink and, as night fell, they came to a delightful glade, in the centre of which stood a little crooked house, ablaze with light. Tired and hungry, Brian dismounted and knocked on the door. It was opened by the oldest man Brian had ever seen. His hair was white as snow and his bushy beard reached down and swept the ground. With twinkling eyes he welcomed his guests. "Céad míle fáilte romhat, Prince Brian of Ireland," he said.

"The south wind whispered that you were on your way. Tell me, why are you here?"

"The Queen, my stepmother, has put geasa on me to bring back water from the Well at the World's End. I am looking for help."

The old man stroked his beard. "I am afraid I cannot help you. I have lived here for two hundred years and, in all that time, two hundred young men have passed this way but not one of them has ever returned. However, I have an older brother who lives a thousand miles along the road. He may be able to help you. Now come in and rest for the night."

A steaming pot of floury potatoes was sitting on the

-- as night fell they came to a delightful glade, in the centre of which stood a little crooked house ----

hearth and, when the travellers had eaten their fill, washed down by mugs of fresh buttermilk, the old man showed them to their beds.

Brian slept soundly and was up with the dawn ready for the journey, but Fergus shrank down under the covers.

"My head aches. My bones are jelly." he stammered. "I have a fever. Let me stay here until you return."

Brian agreed for, truth to tell, he was glad to be rid of his cowardly stepbrother.

When Brian was leaving, the old man gave him a silver spool of thread.

"Throw this before you on the road and follow where it leads. You will meet many dangers. You will be scorched by the sun and frozen by the wind. Demon spirits will mock you and try to lead you astray. Do not look to right or left. Keep your eyes on the thread and success will be yours. Go n-éirí an bóthar leat."

A narrow, winding path led from the house, through the wood and across the meadow. Brian followed the path over the hills, and trees and thorns seemed to open up before him. As he pressed on, finding his way with difficulty through the forest, it grew darker and darker. He began to hear voices that mocked him. He saw demons peering at him from the trees. But he never looked to right or left and, at length and at long last when he thought he could go no further, the silver spool came to rest at the foot of a giant oak tree that stood in the middle of the forest.

To Brian's amazement a door in the tree swung open and out stepped an old, old man with snow white hair and a bushy beard that reached down and swept the ground.

"Fáilte Uí Cheallaigh romhat, Prince Brian of Ireland.

The swallows told me to expect you. Why are you here?"

When Brian finished his story the old man gave a sigh that echoed like thunder through the forest.

"Five hundred years I have lived in this place and, in all that time, five hundred warriors have passed this way. Not one of them has ever returned. However, my older brother – who lives two thousand miles along the road – may be able to help you."

That night Brian feasted on the fruits of the forest: wild strawberries, bilberry pie, honey from the comb, sweet nectar.

As dawn was breaking, the old man climbed out of the tree and whistled loud and clear. A black cloud passed overhead and a golden eagle, with a mighty wingspan, dropped to the ground.

"You are a brave young man, Brian, and you have come through terrible hardships but these are as nothing compared with what you will meet; icy mountains, where the cold is so intense that your blood can turn to ice; raging volcanoes, forests of fire, flames that lick the moon and the stars. Do not look to left or right. Keep tight hold of the eagle and success will be yours. May luck go with you."

Brian climbed up on the eagle's back and the mighty bird soared into the sky. They passed over the Mountain of Perpetual Snow, the icy breath of which seemed to slip into his body and chip off the insides of his bones. They crossed the Valley of the Goblins, where Brian could see large furnaces of fire and smoke. Thousands

and thousands of goblins were busy making gold. They flew over the Burning Forest, where the heat was intense. Fierce tongues of flame danced and leaped into the sky, licking the crimson clouds. However, Brian never looked to left or right and, at length and at long last, the Golden Eagle came to rest beside a gleaming white house, right at the edge of the great ocean.

This time the door was opened by the oldest man in the world. He had snow white hair and his bushy beard reached down and swept the ground.

"Ta fíor-chaoin fáilte romhat, Prince Brian of Ireland. The stars peeped out last night and told me you were on your way." he boomed.

"I have come through rain and snow, through frost and flame, searching for the Well at the World's End."

"A thousand years I have lived in this place and, in all that time, a thousand princes have passed this way. Not one has ever returned. However, you are a brave and kind young man and I shall help you all I can."

That night Brian feasted on wild salmon rubbed with garlic and anointed with honey and drank honey mead.

In the morning the old man led him down to the seashore. He took off his shoe and threw it into the water. A white mist rose from the sea. When it disappeared, Brian saw a little boat in the shape of a shoe rocking on the waves.

"This little boat will take you to the World's End, but you will have a long way to go to complete your journey. I have sent my little brown donkey ahead to guide you along. The castle at the World's End, where you will find the Well, is guarded by a thousand beasts and a thousand guards. Once every hundred years all within sleep for one hour. As miraculous luck would have it, that hour is fast approaching. If you hurry you may reach the castle in time."

Brian kissed the old man goodbye and stepped into the boat. In less time than it takes in the telling he had landed at the World's End. A shaggy old donkey, with great drooping eyes, was waiting on the shore. He gave the animal a big hug and jumped up on its back. They went the high roads and the byroads. They passed big cities that were gay with music and life, and small villages that were wrapped in slumber and silence. They passed over great deserts and wonderful plains. They travelled on and on, without stay or rest, until at long last they came in sight of a beautiful white castle built of marble inset with gleaming stones.

The castle was guarded by a seven-headed dragon, which breathed fire and brimstone out of each of its seven mouths, and a thousand savage beasts which shook the skies with their roars. As Brian approached, midnight struck and every living creature within the castle walls fell fast asleep.

Brian rode in through the golden gates and filled his bottle from the well.

"As I've come this far I might as well go farther," thought Brian as he crossed the courtyard. He entered a long hall where guards were drawn up in rows, snoring for all they were worth.

Finally, he came to a golden room where the walls and ceiling and floor were covered with large emeralds, set closely together. A great throne of green marble stood in the centre of the room and on it lay a lovely girl whose beauty shone with unearthly radiance. Trembling, Brian bent down and kissed her. He took a ring from his finger and placed it on her hand.

As Brian reached the golden gates, all within the castle sprang back to life. Just in time, he leaped on the donkey's back and the brave animal wasted no time until it arrived at the water's edge. Before stepping into the boat, Brian gave the donkey a drop of the water he had taken from the Well at the World's End and its shaggy coat became sleek and silky, and its tired eyes shone like diamonds.

On his journey home Brian gave each of the three old men a drop of the water and in turn their hair turned black, their backs straightened and they became young and handsome and full of life.

When the beautiful Princess from the World's End awoke, she set out for Ireland in search of Brian.

"You stole my heart," she told the young Prince.

"And I left you my ring," he replied.

Very soon after, the young couple were married. The wedding was the best ever seen. The little brown donkey drew the golden coach with the Prince and Princess inside and the three brothers were the guests of honour. The feasting and merriment lasted for a year and a day and the last day was better than the first.

As for the Queen, she was so excited to get the water from the Well at the World's End, and so relieved to have the two young princes safely back home, that she vowed for ever more to be on her best behaviour. And, strange to tell, she kept her promise.

The Gobán Saor

Long ago, longer than I could tell you, and twice as long as you could tell me, there lived in Ireland a master builder known as the Gobán Saor

Now this Gobán Saor had a son called Eoin, a fine handsome youth with black, curly hair and dancing blue eyes.

His best friends were a bushy-tailed fox, called Rua; a cat with no tail, called Gearr; and a red-feathered hen with a limp, called Circín. All three pets got on remarkably well together. Each day they went out with Eoin, hunting on the mountains or fishing in the rivers. Not that they ever caught, trapped or snared anything but they enjoyed themselves and had fun.

Children laughed, and old folk shook their heads in amazement, as the friends went by, the fox leading the way with the cat seated on its back and the hen perched on the cat's head, with Eoin trotting behind. It was a sight to marvel at.

Some people thought that Eoin was not very bright but there is more to wisdom than school books or learning to add and subtract, important as these things are. Eoin was wise in the ways of the wild. For instance, he knew where the golden eagle nested, where the wise salmon rested

RC Gates '90

under a stone in the river, and where the leprechaun hid his crock of gold. He also knew the language of animals: fish and fowl and good red herrings.

But time passed, as it must for all of us. The day came when his father, the Gobán Saor, thought it time for Eoin to marry a girl with brains who could guide and direct him in the way he should go. The Gobán Saor was the first man in Ireland to remark that behind every successful man is a clever wife. And never was there a truer saying, as any mother will tell her son.

The way he decided to bring this about was to send Eoin to the fair with a sheep, telling him to bring back the animal *and* its price.

"Indeed and you have set me an impossible task," Eoin complained, but his father was set in his ways, so off the boy went.

When he reached the fair and told his tale, he was laughed out of the place.

"Is it let you keep the animal and give you its price?" mocked strong farmers and cattle drovers and the like.

And some bullies pelted Eoin with stones, and women said that he should not be let out on his own.

Feeling shamed and saddened, Eoin took the road home, driving the sheep before him. At the corner of a boreen, Rua the fox suddenly popped out of his den and barked, "Follow me". His bushy tail led Eoin to a pretty thatched cottage where a young girl sat spinning outside the half-door.

She smiled at Eoin and said, "What's your name?"

He twisted and turned – for he was woefully shy with girls with long golden hair and big blue eyes – and confessed who he was. Then, summoning up all his courage, he asked her, "What's *your* name?"

"Fionnuala" she said and smiled again. They might still be standing there looking at each other if Gearr, the-cat-with-no-tail, had not appeared.

"Ask her to solve the puzzle," she miaowed.

"About the sheep and its price," prompted Rua, the fox.

"But first, give her a little gift," crowed Circín, the red-feathered hen, and promptly laid a big brown egg which Eoin presented to Fionnuala with a bow. Things were looking up.

"What's your problem, Eoin dear?" Fionnuala asked.

"My father sent me out with this sheep you see grazing in your field. He ordered me to bring home the animal *and* its price."

"You can keep your sheep and I'll give you its price," Fionnuala said promptly, "and it will be a fair bargain."

And with that she took down a pair of shears and sheared the sheep of its wool. Then she gave Eoin a golden guinea and sent him home with the shorn animal.

The Gobán Saor was well pleased when he heard Eoin's story. "That's the wife for you," he decided and the pair were married. The Gobán built them a fine house and, as for the wedding, the last day was better than the first, though the feast lasted all of a month.

Now some time later, the King of the Western World sent for the Gobán to build him a castle. " I'll take you with me," the Gobán said to Eoin, "if you promise to shorten the road on our journey."

"How can I do that?" Eoin asked his wife, Fionnuala, before he set out with his father.

"Easy enough," she smiled. "All you have to do is to chat him up and tell him some stories. That way the time will pass and the road will shorten."

So Eoin, who had a wonderful imagination, told his father marvellous tales about a giant who could crack coconuts with his teeth, and a wise woman who could recite spells backwards, and a poor man who found an enchanted pot which never emptied: the more he ate, the bigger grew the pot. He also knew the story of the King of the Glass Mountains and about the wonderful voyage of Bran and how he met mermaids and monsters of the sea and came home again safe and well.

Before they knew it, they had reached the King of the Western World and the Gobán, with the help of his son Eoin, spent a year and a day building the finest castle ever seen. However, the King was wily and wise in the ways of the world and he determined that neither the Gobán nor his son, Eoin, would ever again build its equal. So he made a plan to keep them prisoners in his dungeon when the last brick was in place.

The Gobán guessed what was afoot. He asked the King's son to fetch him special tools which he needed to finish the job.

"Go back the road to the house where my daughter-in-law, Fionnuala, lives. Tell her I need the glass hammer and a special screwdriver called Twist for Crookedness."

When the young Prince arrived and gave Fionnuala the message, she immediately guessed its meaning. There is no such tool as a glass hammer and the Twist for Crookedness meant that the King was planning mischief.

So Fionnuala knew that she must think harder than ever.

"Go down to the cellar and fetch the tools," she told the Prince. No sooner had she him trapped than she bolted the cellar door and sent word to the King that she would exchange one for two.

The King was no fool and he well knew what she meant. His one son for her two men, husband and father-in-law. He released the Gobán and Eoin and gave them a bag of gold for their trouble. As soon as they arrived safely home, Fionnuala allowed the young Prince to go free.

And so it was that the fame of the Gobán Saor, his son Eoin and his clever daughter-in-law, Fionnuala, spread throughout the land. And if they didn't deserve it, who did? That's my story for you.

The Cattle Raid of Cooley

Long, long ago, when Cúchulainn was just a boy of seventeen, Ailill and Maeve were King and Queen of Connacht. Maeve was tall and beautiful, with twisted yellow tresses, green eyes and cheeks flushed like the foxglove. For charm and courage she had no equal in Ireland, nor indeed in any country in the Western World.

Maeve had a pet squirrel which she always carried high on her shoulders and, on cold winter mornings when Maeve led the hunt,the squirrel would wrap his long bushy tail around her neck and keep her snug and warm.

One dark night, when Maeve and Ailill were relaxing after a hard day's hunting, Maeve boasted that she had more possessions than her husband. Now Ailill was a very proud man and he naturally denied that this was true. So the King and Queen decided to take stock of all they possessed.

They counted their household goods: wooden cups and bowls, iron vessels, basins, pots and cauldrons. They compared their treasures: precious stones, diamonds, amethysts, emeralds and bracelets, necklets and brooches. They took out all their clothes: magnificent garments of many colours, yellow, light blue, dark blue, green, white and crimson. They listed all their animals: vast herds of cattle, sheep, deer, hare and wild boar.

Each time, they found their possessions were equal. Maeve had bright silver combs, ornamented with gold and studded with the rarest emeralds. Ailill matched these with knives and daggers with blades of patterned gold and handles inlaid with diamond and priceless sapphires.

Maeve had a rare purple wool cloak, lined with the purest wild silk but Ailill equalled this with a handsome tunic of fine linen, interwoven with pure gold thread. And so the counting and checking went on. Only in one thing did Maeve and Ailill differ.

The King had a White Bull called Finnbheannach. Finnbheannach was a fierce creature with the strength and size of fifty bulls. Its huge horns were decorated with bright silver, and a silver ring the size of a cart wheel was threaded through its enormous snout. It was so broad that fifty boys could play hurling on its back and the full herd of cattle could shelter beneath it. While its musical lowing would lull even the most stubborn cows to sleep, its snorting and bellowing, when angry, sounded like thunder rolling across the great central plain of Ireland.

Maeve had no bull to equal this fine animal. Indeed there was only one bull in the whole of Ireland which could compare with Ailill's White Bull – a Brown Bull which was owned by Daire Mac Fiachna, a chieftain who lived in Cooley in Ulster.

Now Daire Mac Fiachna was a generous man. When Maeve sent her messengers to Ulster to ask him for the loan of the Brown Bull in exchange for rich rewards and gifts, Daire was very happy to give her the bull. He made the messengers very welcome and the choicest of food and drink was set before them.

All went well until Maeve's messengers got drunk and, as the Irish saying goes, 'Nuair a bhíonn an t-ól istigh bíonn an chiall amuigh' – Drink dulls the senses. One of the Connacht men stupidly boasted that, had Daire not agreed to give the bull freely, it would have been taken by force.

When Daire heard this, he was furious. He sent the messengers scurrying back to Maeve to tell her that he would never part with the bull. Maeve immediately marshalled her army to march against Ulster to take the Brown Bull of Cooley by force.

With her pet squirrel on her shoulder and her golden hair blowing in the wind, Maeve rode at the head of her army. She crossed the Shannon at Athlone and there pitched her camp.

At this time in history, a troop of expert soldiers known as the Red Branch Knights defended Ulster for their king, Conor MacNessa. The warriors of the Red Branch Knights were known throughout the length and breadth of Ireland for their fearless deeds. Alas, when Maeve invaded Ulster, they had been stricken by a strange sleeping sickness which affected them every year at the coming of winter. This magical sickness was the result of a spell cast on King Conor and his soldiers by the angry goddess Macha because the King had scorned her. Cúchulainn had escaped the sickness because he was not in Ulster when the goddess cast her spell. Now Cúchulainn, singlehanded, was left to defend Ulster against Queen Maeve and her army.

Day after day, without rest or sleep, Cúchulainn faced the enemy and no man who came to do battle with him

escaped with his life. Hundreds of Connacht warriors lay slaughtered on the battlefield so that the waters of the river turned to deep crimson.

Cúchulainn would not have had the will to continue the fight but for his pet boar who stayed faithfully by his master's side. When the champion's body was torn and bleeding after the day's battle, his faithful boar healed the wounds by licking them clean. When Cúchulainn felt too weak to face the enemy, his bristly servant nudged him with its snout and calmed him with sweet music such as could not be excelled by a lark or a blackbird.

Then one day a great cry of fear went up from the men of Connacht. No man could be found to face Cúchulainn, the Hound of Ulster. Maeve sent for Ferdia, the only warrior who could match Cúchulainn in valour. Now Cúchulainn and Ferdia loved each other like brothers; they had grown up together and together they had learned the art of war from Scathach, the woman warrior in the Isle of Skye. So Ferdia refused to fight Cúchulainn. Maeve tried to cajole him with promises of great wealth and land. She even offered him her beautiful daughter, Finnabair, in marriage but Ferdia was not tempted. When Maeve saw that Ferdia could not be won over by flattery or bribes, she poisoned his heart with lies.

"Cúchulainn says that you are a coward. You are afraid to face him," she told Ferdia.

At first Ferdia would not believe Maeve's lies but, little by little, his love for Cúchulainn turned to hate and at last he agreed to fight his best friend.

Cúchulainn was heartbroken when he saw Ferdia

advancing to meet him. He begged his friend not to fight but Ferdia's heart was hardened. "The time for talking is over. We shall fight to the end."

The heroes were equally matched. For three days spears flew from side to side with such speed that many onlookers were blinded by the brightness of the blades.

When the first long day was over, Cúchulainn and Ferdia threw down their weapons, waded into the river and kissed and hugged. That night their horses shared the same paddock and their charioteers sat around the same fire. Cúchulainn sent Ferdia special herbs and magic potions to heal his wounds and Ferdia shared his food with Cúchulainn.

On the second day, the heroes fought from their chariots and, when evening came, they again embraced as before. That night their horses shared the same paddock and their charioteers sat around the same fire. Cúchulainn sent Ferdia healing potions and Ferdia shared his food with Cúchulainn.

On the third day, the warriors faced each other across the river. From the early morning until the moth hour of night, the spears were thrown so fast that they were like the flash of swallows' wings. But when the day drew to a close the friends did not kiss or embrace or show any other sign of friendship. That night their horses did not share the same paddock, nor did the charioteers sit around the same fire.

It was with heavy hearts that the champions came to the river on the fourth day. Each knew that the end was in sight. Before nightfall, one of them must die.

Ferdia was the swifter of the two. He caught his opponent off guard so that the blade of his sword burned into Cúchulainn's breast and pinned him to the ground. But, quick as a flash, Cúchulainn's pet boar was at his side and, with one mighty tug, he pulled the sword from his master's body and licked the wound.

Cúchulainn then called for his Gae Bolga – his magical spear, which had been given to him by the people of the Shee. He took careful aim and the spear shot through the air with such hissing and screaming that it left behind a trail of fire. It struck Ferdia with such force that it cut through his iron armour and pierced his noble heart. With a mighty leap, Cúchulainn was at Ferdia's side. He caught him as he fell and carried his dying friend across the river so that he might die in Ulster.

No moonlight showed and even the stars were dimmed as a great silence fell on the land. Ferdia, hero of Connacht, foster-brother of Cúchulainn, was dead.

While the battle was taking place, Maeve's warriors invaded Ulster and carried the Brown Bull of Cooley back to her palace where it was put to graze with Finnbheannach, the King's White Bull. The Brown Bull of Cooley was angry at being held prisoner in Connacht, the White Bull was furious because his territory was threatened. Their eyes blazed like balls of fire. A fierce and terrible fight broke out between the two; they made the hard ground soft and the soft ground dust. When the dust finally settled the Brown Bull of Cooley was seen galloping northwards with the torn body of the White Bull on its horns. As it reached Cooley, it gave a final bellow of triumph and collapsed in death.

Meanwhile, the warriors of Ulster awoke from their enchantment; when they saw Ferdia dead and

Cúchulainn grief stricken, they let out three great shouts and attacked Maeve's soldiers. They killed ten thousand warriors in a single day and, chanting a victory song, they drove Maeve's soldiers back to Connacht. And so ended the Cattle Raid of Cooley.

Deirdre and the Sons of Usna

It was Midsummer's Eve and, from every hilltop in Ireland, bonfires blazed.

Conor Mac Nessa, King of Ulster, with his Red Branch Knights was celebrating the festival in the house of Feilimidh, the King's storyteller. A great crowd had gathered in the banqueting hall around a huge fire burning in the centre of the room. The king sat on a raised dais and, all around him in order of rank, the nobles and warriors of Ulster lay on their couches.

Feilimidh's servants carved mighty joints of venison, sides of beef and roast suckling pigs. They filled goblets to overflowing from vast vats of ale and mead. Beside each man was a dish of honey and another of salt to flavour the meats.

Now it happened that Feilimidh's wife had recently given birth to a beautiful baby girl. When all had eaten their fill, the King raised his drinking horn and called for a toast to the baby's future.

At this command the assembled multitude rose. Only one lone, dark figure solemnly remained seated.

"What means this insult?" thundered Conor Mac Nessa. "Who dares ignore the King's command?"

A hush fell on the hall. Cathbad, the wisest druid in the kingdom, had incurred the king's wrath.

"Why sit you there, dark druid, on this most joyful occasion?" demanded the King.

"What means this insult
Who
dares ignore the Kings
command ?

Cathbad sighed deeply. When he spoke, fear entered the hearts of even the bravest warriors.

"I congratulate Feilimidh on the birth of his daughter but I have looked into the future and have seen the destruction and desolation that this child will bring to the kingdom."

"She shall be called Deirdre and her beauty shall be legendary. Great kings and noble warriors shall strive for her love. Evil shall come from her."

When the men of Ulster heard the words of doom they cried, "let the child of Feilimidh die."

But Conor would have none of it.

"No harm shall befall this child. She shall be taken from this place to the lonely hills and reared where no eye but mine shall see her beauty. In time I will take her to be my wife."

And so it happened that Deirdre grew up in a solitary rath in the hollow hills, her only companions her foster parents and Leabharcham, her nurse.

With each passing year Deirdre grew more beautiful with skin soft and delicate as the rose, eyes blue as the cornflower, hair golden as the ripe corn in the meadow.

Each year, on her birthday, Conor visited Deirdre and brought her priceless gifts: splendid cloaks, gold and silver combs for her hair, sapphire and ruby rings. But Conor was now old and grey and Deirdre, young and beautiful, could never love him.

She had no playmates but her favourite horse, Dubh, that shared all her secrets.

One day she saw her foster father skin a calf. Snow decorated the trees and covered the ground, which was stained by the blood of the calf. From an oak a raven, black as soot, flew down to drink the blood.

“The man I marry,” she whispered in the horse’s ear as they galloped over the hills, “will have hair as black as the raven, skin whiter than snow and cheeks blood red as the berries of the mountain ash in Autumn.” And Dubh turned his head and gave a warning neigh. For a horse has a sixth sense and it knew that Deirdre’s dreams were doomed.

King Conor planned to wed Deirdre on her sixteenth birthday. As the fatal day drew near, she became wan and listless, refusing to eat. Each time she thought of what lay ahead, tears filled her eyes.

“I cannot marry the King,” she confided in Leabharcham, her nurse. “In my dreams I see the one I must love. He is handsome and strong and kind.”

“There is only one such man in the whole of Ireland,” answered Leabharcham. “He is Naoise, one of the Sons of Usna.”

Deirdre begged Leabharcham to bring Naoise to her and, at first, the nurse refused, fearing Conor’s anger. But Deirdre fretted and grew ill so that it seemed that she must surely die from heartbreak. In the end, Leabharcham sent for Naoise.

When Naoise looked at Deirdre, he was spellbound by her beauty. When Deirdre heard the sweetness of Naoise’s voice and saw the loveliness of his face, she knew that he was the only man she could ever love.

Naoise knew full well that Conor had sworn to kill whoever would bewitch his bride-to-be. So, with his brothers Ainle the Fair and Ardan the Ruthless, the young couple left their beloved Ulster and set out on their wanderings.

For a long time they travelled on horseback throughout the length and breadth of the land. But, wherever they went, Conor's soldiers pursued them. When there was no place left for them to hide, they turned their backs on Ireland and set sail for Scotland.

Scotland was a wild, unwelcoming country but the fame of the Sons of Usna as huntsmen and warriors had gone before them and the King of Scotland took them into his service.

Naoise built a house in the deep woods and covered the roof and sides with rushes so that Deirdre was hidden from sight.

For a time they were happy. By day, Deirdre occupied herself with household duties, baking meats and bread, brewing mead from wild honey and hazel nuts, or just wandering through the woods. Birds came to feed from her hands. She tamed wild deer and the red fox and caught salmon and trout with her bare hands. By night, she lay close to Naoise under the stars and talked of the day they could return home once more.

One summer's day, when Naoise was away hunting, Deirdre ventured far into the woods. She was paddling her feet in a tumbling brook when the King of Scotland passed by. Deirdre had never looked lovelier. Her hair shone like burnished gold and, around her shoulders, she wore a crimson cloak. The King was bewitched by her beauty and, there and then, decided to marry her. When Naoise heard this, he knew that he must leave Scotland or face death.

At the dead hour of night, Deirdre and the Sons of Usna left their home in the woods and sought refuge on a bleak and barren island off the coast of Scotland. Food was scarce and they were tired from wandering. They could not stay in Scotland, neither did they dare return to Ireland.

One day Fergus Mac Roy, an Ulster chieftain and loyal friend to the Sons of Usna, came on a mission to the island. He brought a message from King Conor. If Deirdre and the Sons of Usna would return home, they would be pardoned and made welcome.

Naoise and his brothers were delighted with the news. Deirdre, however, mistrusted Conor. Her dreams of home and been troubled. Naoise calmed her. For as long as they were under the protection of Fergus, no harm would come to them. And so it happened that, gathering up their belongings, they sailed back to Ireland.

When they reached the coast of Antrim they set out at once for Emain Macha, for Naoise had sworn not to eat or rest on the journey until he reached home. However, by a clever ruse, Conor arranged that they were no longer in the safe keeping of Fergus. He told Borrach, his chieftain, to invite Fergus to a meal. Now Fergus was under bonds never to refuse any hospitality offered. So, reluctantly, he remained in Antrim while Deirdre and the Sons of Usna travelled on to Emain Macha without the protection of their champion and friend.

Now it happened that Conor had just concluded a peace treaty with Eogán, a long standing enemy and, in return for cattle and gold, Eogán pledged to kill the Sons of Usna.

When Deirdre, Naoise and his brothers reached

the Sons of Usna fought valiantly.

Emain Macha, they were surprised that Conor was not waiting to welcome them on the ramparts of his palace. Instead they were ambushed by Eogán and his warriors and, though the Sons of Usna fought valiantly, by nightfall they lay dead on the battlefield. Deirdre was taken to Conor, who still hoped to marry her, but her heart had died with Naoise. She never smiled or spoke again.

Exactly one year later, Deirdre was riding in the chariot with Conor. As they passed the spot where her beloved Naoise had been killed, Deirdre rose up in her seat and threw herself from the speeding chariot. She dashed her head against a rock and died.

That Spring an oak tree grew on the spot where Deirdre died and, year after year, to this very day, two white doves nest in its lofty branches.

How Fionn became leader of The Fianna

Did you ever hear how Fionn became leader of the Fianna? It is a story well worth the telling, so draw a chair up to the fire and listen carefully.

Long, long ago, Ireland was ruled by a High King, called Cormac Mac Airt, who lived in great splendour in his castle at Tara in County Meath.

The King had a band of warriors, called the Fianna, brave and fearless soldiers who protected the country against invaders. Their main fort was on the Hill of Allen in County Kildare. When they weren't fighting the King's enemies – or entertaining the court with sweet music, poetry and wonderful stories of their heroic exploits – they loved to hunt the wild boar and red deer throughout the deep valleys and great forests of Ireland.

Fair-haired Fionn, handsome and a giant among men, was the most famous leader of the Fianna. But, at this point in time, Fionn was only a baby and his father, Cumhail of Clann Baoisne, was its captain. Cumhail was a good soldier and a great leader but his enemies, the Sons of Morna, were jealous of his power and influence with the High King. They felt that Goll Mac Morna should be leader. They schemed and connived, they plotted and planned Cumhail's downfall. Finally, at the Battle of Cnucha (Castleknock – near where Dublin's Phoenix Park is today), the rebellious Sons of Morna killed Cumhail and Goll Mac Morna became the new leader of the Fianna. The sons of Morna took Cumhail's

treasure bag which held his magic cap, his special spear and the drinking horn which had been given to him by the fairies. As long as they had this bag, Goll Mac Morna would remain leader of the Fianna.

After Cumhail's death, Fionn's mother knew that it

was only a matter of time before the Sons of Morna would seek out and kill her baby son. So, although it broke her heart, she gave him into the care of two women warriors who lived deep in a wood on the slopes of Sliabh Bloom in County Laois.

From an early age, Fionn showed great promise as a warrior and a leader. His friends and companions were the wild animals and birds of the forest and, from them, he learned how to run and jump and swim and forage for food. In no time at all he could outrun the wind, the swallow and the deer and, armed with only a stick and a shield, he could defend himself against a dozen men throwing spears at him from close range.

Fionn loved the Wise Women of Sliabh Bloom and he loved his animal friends. Nothing gave him more pleasure than to roam through the forest at the first light of dawn and listen to the sweet song of the blackbird, or play hide and seek with the cotton-tailed rabbits. But he knew that one day he must take his rightful place as leader of the Fianna so, with his faithful hound, Bran, at his heels and his spear and shield on his arm, he set out to recover his father's treasure bag.

Fionn had the strength of five hundred warriors and as a hunter he had no equal. Everywhere he went, men spoke in hushed tones of this fairhaired giant who had the walk of a king but who dressed in wild boar skins and sandals of untanned oxhide.

He travelled all over Ireland searching for the warriors who had stolen his father's treasures. However, as the days grew into months and the months into years, Fionn lost hope. He became despondent because,

without the magic bag, he could never become leader of the Fianna.

On a fine summer morning, when Fionn was fishing the river Shannon, Bran came bounding up, very excited, and dropped the treasure bag at his master's feet. Before Fionn had time to draw his breath, the most fearsome creature he had ever seen came thundering up behind the dog.

Fionn stood up from the bank and eyed the newcomer. "And who might you be and what is your business?"

"I am one of the Sons of Morna," the giant roared. "This wretched hound of yours has stolen my treasure bag."

"Even as you stole it from my father," Fionn said and drew his sword as the giant lunged at him.

The battle that followed lasted for three days and three nights before Fionn could declare himself the victor.

Now that he had the treasure bag, Fionn turned his mind to poetry for, as you know, every member of the Fianna had to learn twelve books of poetry by heart. With his four-legged friend at his side, he set out for the Boyne Valley where the sun always shines, the bees produce the sweetest honey and the six best poets in Ireland lived.

It was when Fionn was studying with Finnéigeas, a wise and great poet, that he tasted the Salmon of Knowledge so that, forever after when he chewed his thumb, he could see into the future. He had the gift of wisdom.

When Fionn had learned all the poetry ever composed and his master could teach him no more, he set his sights on Tara.

It was November Eve, the time of year when the fairy mounds of Ireland are open and the People of the Otherworld roam the earth.

As was customary at this time of year, the High King entertained the wise and the noble, the skilful and the brave in his magnificent palace at Tara. The four great roads which ran north, south, east and west from Tara to the four corners of Ireland were thronged with poets and kings, jesters and druids, jugglers and musicians, each bearing a special gift for the High King.

Night was falling when Fionn reached Tara, but flames from huge bonfires reached up to the stars and lit up the palace, outlining the magnificent columns of bronze.

When Fionn entered the great banqueting hall the feast was ready. An enormous oak table groaned under the weight of food and drink – roast succulent pig, haunches of beef, venison, smoked hams, cheese, wheaten cakes cooked in honey, blackberries, apples, nuts, pitchers of milk, jugs of mead, casks of fine wine and barrels of ale.

On a raised dais sat the High King and around him the four provincial kings, resplendent in rich robes, and the mighty men of the Fianna: Goll Mac Morna, Conán Maol, Caoilte Mac Ronáin, Diarmuid Mac Duibne.

Yet, though it was a great feast and vessels of gold, silver and bronze sparkled under the light of many torches, an air of gloom and doom prevailed. Every year, on November Eve, the Lord of the Underworld appeared at Tara and burned the palace to the ground.

To protect it from destruction, the High King ringed the palace with his bravest and best warriors each year, but in vain. As the Lord of the Underworld approached Tara he played slow, sweet, enchanting music on a magic flute so that all who heard it fell into a deep slumber. Then, as they slept, he blew a ball of fire from his nostrils and everything that the fire touched was destroyed.

The King spoke: "Is there any man among you who will defend Tara this night?"

At first, a hushed silence fell on the assembly. In the past, brave men had tried, in vain, to save Tara and had been shamed for life.

Then Fionn stood up: "What will you give me, your majesty, if I defend the palace?"

"Whatever is most dear to your heart," said the King.

Fionn clashed his shield. "I am Fionn, son of the mighty Cumhail. I have come to Tara to claim my rightful place as leader of the Fianna."

Goll Mac Morna let out a cry and drew his sword but was silenced by the King.

"Fionn, son of Cumhail, I give you my pledge. Save Tara and the leadership of the Fianna is yours."

As midnight drew near, Fionn left the great hall. He crossed the outer ramparts of the palace on to the wide plain stretching out below. The bonfires had died down and the sky was black. Nothing stirred. On November Eve it is not safe to be out of doors.

As midnight struck, the fairy mound that stands on the hill of Tara opened and the ugliest man Fionn had ever seen stepped out. He was twenty feet tall, as thin as a reed and he was playing slow, sweet, sad music on his magic flute. Fionn's eyes began to close. He fought off sleep. Just in time he remembered to chew on his thumb. At once he knew what he must do. He took the magic cap out of his treasure bag and put it on his head. Wonder of wonders, he was wide awake. The spell was broken. As Fionn watched, wide-eyed, the Lord of the Underworld blew a huge ball of fire from his nostrils, aimed at the palace. Fionn stepped out of the shadows and caught and quenched the fireball in his great cloak. A second time the creature blew a ball of fire from his nostrils and again it was caught and quenched.

Without his magic, the Lord of the Underworld was

powerless. He turned towards the fairy mound. Quick as lightning, Fionn aimed his magic spear. It shot through the air and pierced the Lord of the Underworld through the heart. There was a deafening scream, a blinding flash and when Fionn looked again the Lord of the

Underworld had vanished. Only scorched earth remained on the spot where the magician had stood.

As Fionn made his way back into the palace, the High King, the Fianna, the provincial kings and their courtiers, the musicians, the jugglers and the palace cooks were awakening from their enchanted sleep. When the Fianna heard of Fionn's wondrous deed, they carried him shoulder high to the King who immediately appointed him their leader.

From that day forward, the Fianna grew in strength and their feats were related with bated breath all over Ireland, as they are to this very day.